art and design
drawing

Chris Dunn

Hodder & Stoughton
A MEMBER OF THE HODDER HEADLINE GROUP

Introduction

Student's work, drawing with wire, a self portrait

The National Curriculum divides the subject of Art and Design into two distinct areas. These areas, known as Attainment Targets are called:
AT 1 – Investigating and Making
AT 2 – Knowledge and Understanding

By the end of Key Stage 4, when you sit your GCSE you should show you have reached certain levels in each of these Attainment Targets. This book will ensure that you have the chance to reach these levels. It does it not by dividing the subject into neat, discrete areas of study but by stressing the nature of Art and Design as a continuous experience.

This book is the first of a series, each of the others deals with a particular materials base so that if you study any of the endorsed papers then you will find an appropriate book. This book deals with drawing, in its widest sense and is a fundamental basis for the series, as drawing is a fundamental activity. Though primarily designed for GCSE, this book will also provide projects for other levels of study, especially if you are studying at college. Artwork is assessed by outcome; that is, by what you do. Each of the projects here can be responded to at a high level: its up to you.

Drawing is the basic tool without which you cannot progress no matter which materials you use. It is also a skill that can be learnt, developed and applied in an individual way. Drawing is of wider importance that just a skill, however well applied. The keeping of a sketchbook is stressed as a continuous record the world around you, an important part of work in any material. Your progress as an artist depends on the habit of keeping a drawn record.

This book will help you consider drawing in its widest sense, it is not only about pencil on paper. This student's drawing is in wire for example. The soft iron wire has been bent and twisted in a continuous line. The self portrait produced is as much a drawing as any pencil and paper exercise.

Throughout this book you will see a wide range of work, by a large variety of artists. The work has been chosen to show you the best examples available in any material. Without doubt any good art library could add to them and hopefully you will feel inspired to go and look for examples yourself. You might like to keep a record of your researches in a scrap or log book in support of each of your projects.

Art is about taking risks: you need to be ambitious. All the projects in this book will stretch your imagination and skills. Each project has been developed so that it could provide the focus of long term research. Each can be extended by your imagination and directed towards its own goals. In this way you will enhance those skills and attainments that the National Curriculum seeks to measure.

Georges Seurat (1851–1891)
Seated Boy with Straw Hat
Conte Pencil, Yale University
Art Gallery

The drawing on this page is by Georges Seurat (1859–1891), can you find out about this important French artist? The very grainy appearance is caused by the artist's use of Conte pencil, a soft greasy pencil that gives a very dark matt effect. In Seurat's work, especially drawings used in preparation for other works, these tonal drawings are created almost without lines at all. This drawing is a study for part of a painting called, *Une Baignade, Asnières* (Bathers at Asnières). This hangs in the National Gallery in London. Contrast this work with the student's work opposite where line is the only element.

Looking at drawings

Almost every piece of art or design work starts life as a drawing, maquette or model. It is the essential first stage between an idea and the finished product. Let us start looking at Art and Design by examining the importance of drawing in our work.

Though pen, pencil and other line media are traditionally associated with drawing, any medium can be used. Often the materials you choose to use depend on the purpose of your drawing. You should decide this before you start to draw. For example, you would be foolish to try and build a piece of machinery if your only preparatory drawings were done with a large paint brush. It is a skill, based on your experience, to choose the most suitable medium. The two artists whose work is shown on these pages show how important this choice is.

Eugene Delacroix (1798–1863) spent many hours in the Paris Zoo drawing caged animals; tigers in particular. His brush drawings from life are a complete explanation of the character of the animal. With simple and economical use of line he has captured the intrinsic spirit of the tiger.

Eugene Delacroix (1798–1863), Tigers. **Brush drawings from life**

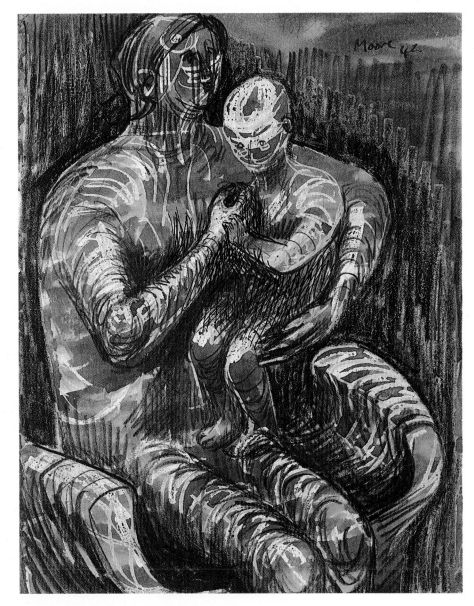

*Draw whenever you can (a
sketchbook is essential) from
observation. Try to avoid
static still life set up without
purpose. It is better to let
drawing follow your curiosity
than be a slave to what can
be easily arranged in the
classroom.*

*Try to expand the range of
techniques that you use. You
might start a list and aim to
add to it each week. This will
help you find techniques that
match the way you use your
drawings.*

*Animals are not usually
patient models. When you are
drawing them you need to
work quickly. You might like
to make a series of drawings
of the family pet or some other
animal. Draw from life, do not
be tempted by photographs or
other artists' work. Try to
discover for yourself a medium
which suits the subject you
are working on.*

Henry Moore (1898–1986) used the fact that wax crayon and water based
paint reject each other to describe the form of the figure in this drawing. He
used the drawing as a preparatory stage in the making of his final piece of
sculpture. Moore used the same technique to describe the huddled form of
sleeping figures in his famous *Shelter Sketchbooks*. These books, drawn while
Moore was an official war artist, show the sleeping figures sheltering in the
London Underground during the Blitz in 1940.

DRAWING

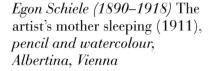

The drawing below shows how more than one medium can be used – in this case pencil and watercolour are used together. Each medium has been chosen for the qualities it can offer. To be able to make this choice, you need as wide a range of drawing experience as possible.

You probably learnt to write quite early in your school career and your writing will have improved with practice. Drawing is a skill and can be learnt in the same way. When you draw you use many of the same abilities that you use when you write. Good co-ordination between hand and eye is essential. You may feel drawing is difficult, but you have learnt many of the basic skills already.

Drawing is essential to both the artist and the designer. It is often the most effective way for them to communicate their ideas. It can help an idea develop. When you draw, you can make real those things you have only imagined. Drawing gives you the flexibility and scope to develop your imagination. These pages will not make you an expert, but they will give you some essential clues so that when you do draw your ideas will develop.

The traditional pencil is probably the most common drawing tool. It comes in many different degrees of hardness; the more usual range from 4H (the hardest) to 6B (the softest). Exceptionally grades up to 9H or down to XXB are available, but these have specialised uses. Rather like the way a wood carver uses different chisel shapes on a carving, so pencil grades each have a different function. Harder pencils are of more value when lines need to be clear and sharp or when measurements need to be taken from them. Softer grades are easier to use for freehand drawing for they need less pressure to leave a mark on the page.

Egon Schiele (1890–1918) **The artist's mother sleeping (1911)**, *pencil and watercolour, Albertina, Vienna*

You might like to experiment with different media, used together. Try oil pastel and watercolour for example or wax crayon and pencil.
Many artists have used members of their own family as subjects for their work. The drawings by Egon Schiele (1890–1918) of his mother asleep and Henry Moore (1898–1986) of his mother are examples of this. Can you find other examples? We often feel more relaxed when working with people we know well. Perhaps this is why these drawings are so successful. You might like to try to produce either a family group or a series of individual dawings of family members

Henry Moore (1898–1986) The Artist's Mother (1927), *pencil, pen and ink, 27.7 × 19.1 cm* © *The Henry Moore Foundation*

Soft pencils leave a trail of graphite dust which can be brushed over with cotton wool, cotton buds or a tissue. Highlights and sharp edges can be defined with a plastic eraser or an eraser pencil. Coloured pencil can be blended with a little duplicator fluid. They can be overdrawn with a white pencil. Colours can be mixed by adding new layers of a different colour. (Use the lightest first then add the darker colours until you have the shade you want.) If you use colour pencils press lightly. A good quality plastic eraser can be used to draw into the coloured shapes. Templates, stencils or even cut paper shapes are all useful to give sharp edges to your drawings.

In some cases water soluble coloured pencils are useful. Simply draw and colour as usual and then use water and a brush to blend colours. The disadvantage is that on all but the heaviest grades, the water deforms the paper.

The three drawings here are examples of how flexible drawing techniques can be; each is successful in its own way. The two on this page are examples of graphic design that use coloured pencil effects to achieve their impact. Can you find examples of coloured pencil used in advertising? In the first advert, white pencil has been used to draw on coloured paper. This can create a dramatic effect, especially when used on black or a dark coloured paper. The white crayon makes use of the paper texture. It has also been used to draw very precise lines. The advertisement dates from 1929 – can you find examples of advertisements that come from the past? Quite frequently the designers of tins or packets are unwilling to drastically alter their designs. One example is the Lyon's 'Golden Syrup' tin, (left). Can you find others?

Advertisement for Chrysler Motors Ltd 1929 designed by Wm. Crawford Ltd (right)

Sports car (the 'Maya') by Ital Design, Turin who are well known for the quality of their illustration work, especially colour rendering on blue paper. This particular design (below) is on blue Ingres paper.

The other example on the opposite page uses a wide variety of media. Drawings of this type are often very large, in some cases life size. These require very specialised skills and may be worked on by more than one artist. This particular drawing is however of more modest size. It is drawn on blue paper with white pencil crayon and white pastel. Darker pencil crayons and pastels are used for the lower surfaces. Marker pens have been used for the reflective surfaces and to give depth to some of the shadows.

The drawing (on the left) can be looked at as mixed media work. The artist did not set out to use as many different media as he could, he had the experience to pick and choose the most effective for the task he wanted to perform. Though the drawing is a sketch to be used in a painting, it has all the qualities of a finished piece of work. Can you find more work from this 15th century Venetian artist? Look at the groups of people he uses in some of his work; you will see why this kind of detailed drawing was important.

Giovanni Bellini (1430–1516)
Portrait of a man with a Turban, *Pen and Ink, chalk and pencil drawn on tinted paper, Uffizi Gallery, Florence*

Almost all design work is based on drawing skills. You must be able to rely on your hands drawing what your eye sees. This hand-eye co-ordination is best developed by drawing from real objects. You can practise this in the studio by drawing individual objects, groups of objects or the human figure from life models. You can also take your skills with you outside. Drawing will give you the quickest, most responsive and flexible record of the world around you.

Sketchbooks

Keith Brockie is a talented young wildlife artist. On his travels he collects information about the natural world. His sketchbook is often worked on in the open air and includes written notes. He uses it for quick sketches, employing a wide variety of media.

Keith lists the contents of the rucksack he takes with him when he draws in the open air. Often long and difficult journeys are required to find the most interesting wildlife sites. It is better not to find that you have left the materials you really need at home. He takes 'a small drawing board, a sketchbook, some artist's board, a selection of ordinary pencils, Conte, ballpoint and felt pens, a half-pan (small size) watercolour box and brushes'.

In addition to working from life he also uses dead (recently dead!) specimens, and occasionally tame birds and animals. He tries to make his drawings as descriptive as possible although, his work is often affected by the weather. You may find it interesting to compare this work with the drawings by Delacroix from his Morocco sketchbook on the cover.

A page from Keith Brockie's Wildlife Sketchbook *showing a cock capercaille*

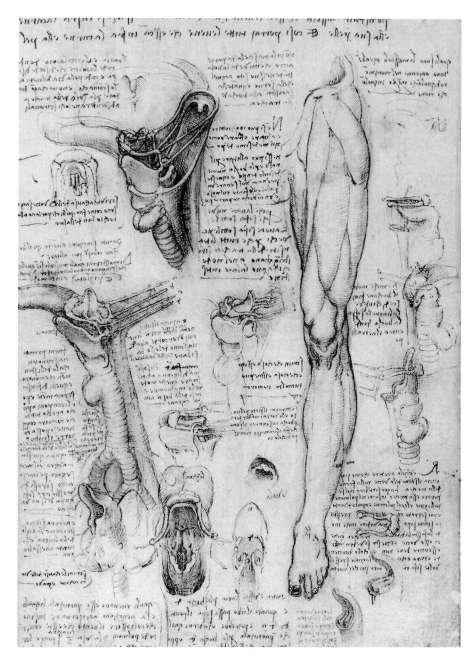

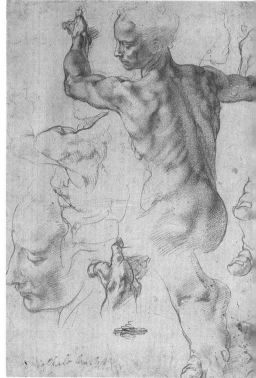

Leonardo da Vinci (1452–1519) Studies of the larynx and the leg, *the Royal Library, Windsor*

Michelangelo Buonarroti (1475–1564), Studies for the painting of the Libyan Sibyl, *part of the Sistine Chapel ceiling, red chalk, Copyright © 1980 Metropolitan Museum of Art*

Leonardo da Vinci was a relentless keeper of notebooks. Driven by a limitless curiosity he made notes on everything that interested him. You might like to look for other examples of his notebook pages. The page shown is a detailed record of the dissections of human bodies that he carried out. Leonardo's investigations of the human body gave him the detailed knowledge that helped him with his figure drawing. This notebook is annotated with his unusual 'mirror' handwriting.

Here the sketchbook is used as a tool in a formal scientific study.

Michelangelo used the sketches (shown right) to work out the details of a figure he used in one of his greatest pieces of work – The Sistine Chapel ceiling in St Peter's, Rome. He sketched the whole figure and then, on different parts of the sheet, he concentrated on areas that he wanted to look at more closely. The drawings on this sheet are an important part in the development of the finished work.

DRAWING

Artists have almost always learnt their craft by developing drawing skills. The drawing by Peter Paul Rubens shows the level of skill that can be reached. It is a finished drawing of a rare landscape, from a time when landscape drawing or painting was usually an excuse for a narrative (story) picture. The materials that Rubens used are very responsive: they give a freedom of expression that is often 'worked out' of more formal paintings. Rubens' landscape paintings rarely approach the freedom of this drawing.

Early artists often learnt by copying existing works; from these copies they progressed to more independent work. Copying work is not encouraged generally, but it can have a place in the preparatory stages of a piece of original work. A finished piece might progress through a series of stages. Firstly through sketches, initially drawn from nature and kept together in a book. Sketches are then developed into studies, usually of details, as in the study opposite by Sir Anthony Van Dyck. A finished drawing combines the initial idea with the detail as revealed by the studies. These distinctions are not often made anymore, though they are still used to catalogue drawings. It is, however, a sensible way to organise your work and you might consider using it. Sketches and studies are an important part of coursework and a valuable resource for your later work. Aim to produce a set amount each week; it is only by being methodical that you will make progress. Make drawing a habit, it will be one you enjoy.

Peter Paul Rubens (1577–1640),
A Path Bordered by Trees,
brown wash on brown paper,
pen and brush, Fitzwilliam
Museum, Cambridge

Sir Anthony Van Dyck (1599–1641) **Study of plants, pen and ink with a brown wash, 21.3 × 32.7 cm, British Museum, London.** *A study drawing, drawn for reference from life*

Sketchbooks: some basics

Learn to draw quickly and with care, think about where your lines are going to go on the page. Learn to draw ahead of the pencil. Draw with economy of line, a few lines well placed will say more than a scrambled ball of indecisive lines.

A pencil is probably the most convenient medium to use out of doors. Remember different grades of pencil are used for different tasks, so take a selection with you. If you have water and a brush then waterbased markers are a good idea. You could do a lot worse than follow the list given by Keith Brockie on page 10. Be careful to use a sheet of card under each page as you draw on it. If you do not the 'ghost' of your drawing could carry through to all the other pages in your sketchbook.

Do not be afraid to use words on your drawings. There may be information that can only be written down. The time of day may be important; you might want to return at the same time to experience the same lighting conditions, for example. Include samples of actual material in your sketchbook if you think it will help you. Feathers, leaves or even pressed flowers collected on the site may help you if you are going to make studies from your sketches in the studio.

These drawings are by Beatrix Potter, best known author of the Peter Rabbit series of children's books. In these tales she gave a collection of everyday animals such as rabbits, mice and pigs human affectations, while retaining their natural characteristics. The first book was written in 1902 (*The Tale of Peter Rabbit*) and the series has proved popular ever since.

The water colour illustrations, though simple, are the result of careful study over many years. Beatrix spent many hours drawing her pet rabbit – called Peter. She also drew museum specimens which helped in her study of anatomy. It is because of this depth of knowledge that her drawings are so successful

You might like to look for other examples of her illustrations. Imagine that you have been given the task of illustrating a page in one of her books. Without copying her illustration, try to bring her illustration up-to-date in technique, style or content

Beatrix Potter (1866–1943)
Study for six heads of rams, pencil, 16.3 × 11.4 cm, copyright © Frederick Warne & Co., 1987

The three drawings here show a variety of approach. Above is a page taken from her sketchbook. The drawings are from life and show how her work developed from careful observation. Through observation she grew to understand the anatomy and behaviour of her subjects.

The second drawing (top, opposite page) is a study. This is a more carefully constructed drawing. It has been drawn from life. It shows a particular sheep and though it may have been quickly drawn it was intended to be a more careful record than a sketch.

Beatrix Potter (1866–1943)
Head of a Sheep, *pencil and watercolour, 12 × 18 cm, copyright © Frederick Warne & Co., 1987*

The drawing (below) may well have started as a sketch from life, but it has been completed in the studio. It is meant to be considered as a finished piece of work. Grisaille is a method of painting using grey tones only.

The drawings here represent the work of the later part of her life when she lived in the Lake District. She took a particular interest in the Herdwick breed of Lakeland sheep.

If you are interested in seeing more of the work of this artist you might like to look at her drawings of fungus and lichen. These can be found in the Victoria and Albert Museum. They are some of the best natural history illustrations available. She studied these subjects for many years and it is this long standing interest that makes her work so striking.

Frequently animals are found in art in association with the human figure. You may be relieved to know that the combination does not always have to be 'cuddly'. You might like to look at other examples of humanised animals going back as far as the animal gods of ancient Egypt.

Beatrix Potter (1866–1943)
Head of a Ram, 1896, *grisaille (painting entirely in tones of grey) with white, 21.8 × 28.8 cm, copyright © Frederick Warne & Co., 1987*

Still life

Still life is the term used to describe a piece of work based on a group of objects. This type of picture is often used by artists to work out ideas or to develop their skills. Traditionally, it includes such things as flowers, fruit, vegetables and other natural objects. It is also common to find manufactured items used in still life groups. Frequently they are made up of objects in common, everyday use in any particular period.

Georges Braque (1882–1963)
Still Life Composition (1912)
Charcoal and collage,
31 × 24 cm, Oeffentliche
Kunstsammlung, Basel,
Martin Bühler.

To be most effective, you need to have a particular interest in the objects you are drawing. You might make a choice from your possessions from home, choose a favourite soft toy or something from a collection. Try to organise objects in a group; their relationships to each other are crucially important

In *Still Life Composition* (left) the objects are difficult to recognise. The artist has shown them from many different angles at the same time. He has left some of them incomplete. Some of the objects are drawn to a different scale. There are examples of real materials included as a part of the drawing. He can do this because he is not trying to show the way the objects really look but wants to tell you as much as he can about the objects. At the same time he wants to give you something interesting to look at.

John Bratby (1928–92)
Still Life with Chip Frier, *1955, oil on board, 12.8 × 9 cm, Tate Gallery, London*

Domenico Cresti Passignano (1559–1638) Garlands of fruit and grotesques, *pen and brown wash, heightened with white, 27.6 × 20.3 cm, British Museum, London*

The avalanche of objects in this painting by John Bratby shows that groups of objects do not have to be organised in a formal way in order to make interesting still life pieces. As a painting, it demonstrates that exciting arrangements can appear informally.

Contrast Bratby's painting with the drawing attributed to the Florentine artist Domenico Cresti Passignano. These garlands of fruit show how groups of objects can be used as decorative elements. You might also like to look at the way Carlo Crivelli (1435–1495) uses fruit and flowers as decorative elements in his work.

Figure

The artist Edgar Degas completed many drawings of ballet dancers. As an artist he was welcomed in their practice rooms and behind the stage. He frequently used his drawings as the basis for large paintings completed later in his studio. He made bronze figures like the one opposite. You should get used to the idea of drawing in preparation for pieces of work. Degas' preparation went further than drawing however, he became absorbed by his subject.

Drawing the human figure requires lots of practice. You might like to choose one of your group to act as a model. To be fair you could take it in turns. Make a series of drawings from different positions around the model. After each drawing make a note of those things you think are wrong with it. On your next drawing try to specifically correct the errors you found earlier. Do not be afraid to be critical; you can only improve when you know what is wrong with your drawings.

Edgar Degas (1834–1917) Study of a Girl Dancer, Suzanne Mante, at the Barre, 1878, *black chalk on pink paper, 34.1 × 24.1 cm, Fitzwilliam Museum, Cambridge*

Edgar Degas (1834–1917) Three Studies of a Dancer in Fourth Position,
c. 1879–80 *charcoal and pastel with stumping, with touches of brush
and black wash, on greyish-tan laid paper with blue fibres (discoloured
pinkish-blue), 48 × 61.5 cm, The Art Institute of Chicago Bequest of
Adele R Levy 1962.703*

His frequent visits to their studios meant that he got to know many of the
dancers and was treated by them as a friend.

The sketches above are in preparation for this piece of bronze sculpture.
Look at the way the artist has altered the drawing to help balance the figure.
Through drawing you can adapt your ideas and alter them to work in different
media.

Edgar Degas (1834–1917), The
Little Dancer, *aged 14, 1881,
Bronze, 98.5 cm × 42 cm ×
36.5 cm, Tate Gallery, London*

Figure Drawing in Context

Hokusai (1760–1849), a page from 'Manga' vol. 8, The Acrobats, *1817. Woodcut, 22.3 × 14.6 cm, British Museum, London*

Etruscan Engraved Mirror showing the Judgement of Paris. 3 BC Bronze, Hirmer Fotoarchiv, Munich

Look at the way that other cultures make drawings of the human figure. Perhaps you could collect examples? You might like to look at the way figure drawing has developed within our own culture.

Can you find examples of the figure in motion?

You might like to try and develop a method of recording movement of your own. If you do it might be interesting to bear in mind the economy of line used by these two artists.

It is interesting to examine these two contrasting pieces of drawing, each from the peak of its particular culture. Both cultures had a strong tradition of figure drawing and you can easily see how the drawings concentrate on the use of line: simple but tellingly accurate. While each is, in a sense, stylized there is no attempt to idealise the subject. The impression is one of movement, of vitality and of incident.

The Etruscan mirror (above) has its roots in the Greek black and red figure-painted pottery. At the time this mirror was made the best pottery came from the Greek colonies on the Italian mainland, neighbours to the Etruscans. The influences are clear; the Etruscan contribution was to strip away the idealisation of the later Greek figures. The figures appear as real people, caught almost unawares. When you consider that the fluid lines of this drawing are engraved with a metal point into hard bronze, then the measure of the artists skill can be appreciated.

Working with an equally difficult medium, Hokusai is heir to the Japanese tradition of woodcuts. These were cut into the soft side-grain of the wood. They can be very complex affairs, using many overprinted blocks, one cut for each colour of the eventual print. These acrobats (left) have the same honesty as the Etruscans. They have been caught unsuspecting at practice and the artist has not attempted to hide their humanity. Hokusai, who called himself 'an old man mad about drawing' produced an unparalleled set of drawings called the 'Manga' a record of his life and times. The 15 volumes contain almost 30 000 drawings.

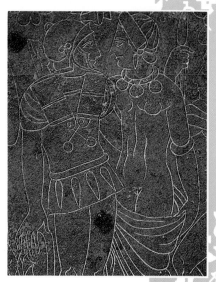

Detail from an Etruscan engraved mirror depicting Helen and Menalaos c.4 BC, bronze, Townley Collection, London British Museum.

Peter Paul Rubens (1577–1640)
Portrait of Helena Fourment,
1630, black and red chalk,
heightened with white, pen and
iron gall ink in the headdress
and in some details in the head,
possibly including later
retouchings. On white laid
paper, 61.2 × 55 cm, Seilern
bequest, 1978, Courtauld

The caption for this drawing has described the techniques used at length so that you can see how complex a drawing of this quality can be. Rubens considered this work, not as a study, but as a completed work. In a finished drawing of this quality the distinction between drawing and painting becomes meaningless.

Contrast the approaches to drawing shown by these two artists. The measured construction of Rubens and the fluid brush work of Tiepolo. The brush stroke used by Tiepolo to create these figures are comparable to the painted lines of the American Abstract Expressionist painter Jackson Pollock.

Giovanni Battista Tiepolo (1698–1779) The Holy Family, *1750, Preliminary drawing in black chalk, pen and brown ink, brush and grey-brown wash, some drawing with the flat and the point of the brush, on thin white laid paper, 28 × 20 cm, Courtauld Institute Galleries*

In both these works a variety of media are used.

You might like to create for yourself a drawing as a finished piece of work. You might like to use different media. Plan and make preliminary studies for your work. Perhaps you could write down in advance what you expect to achieve. This could be written in the form of a 'statement of intent'. You may feel this is a useful exercise since it gives you a measure against which to judge the finished product.

Scrapbook

You might like to look at the work of artists who have created Beastiaries. These are illustrated books of animals, often together with poetry. Pablo Picasso (1881–1973) produced one with the poet Apollinaire (1880–1918). Perhaps you can find others?

Two pages from the Pepysian Sketchbook, Magdalene College, Cambridge

It might seem strange to include a book of drawings under the heading *Scrapbook*. These drawings are a collection made over a long period of time by many different artists. They were collected together between two covers rather as you might collect published and original material in a scrapbook. The *Pepysian Sketchbook* is a 14th century artists' pattern book. It was used by an artists' workshop as a source of decorative ideas. These were used for illuminated manuscripts, paintings, metalwork embroidery and even, perhaps, stained glass.

Many of the creatures included in these works are imagined, though some of the birds may have been drawn from life.

Antonio Pisanello (c.1395–1455)
Saddled Mule in Profile, *Louvre Paris*

The great cathedrals of the 13th and 14th centuries were often covered in carvings. The masons and stone carvers frequently worked from pattern books. By careful measurement of the drawings, using callipers and the skill of the craftsmen, the drawings could be copied. Often the architect brought pattern books with him of his own or collected works. The client, in the case of the church, a bishop or abbot, could select carvings from the book. Catalogue shopping is not a new concept!

In the 13th century this type of pattern book was also used by the makers of 'Opus Anglicum'. This was a very fine embroidery style for which England was famous. It was highly prized for church vestments. Many examples still survive, including some articles made for the Pope.

The drawing below is by the northern Italian artist, Antonio Pisanello (c.1395–1455). This is one of a large number of animal drawings drawn from life. Pisanello was one of the first artists to make his own sketchbook with subjects drawn from life. (Can you find other examples of drawings of animals by this artist?) He used drawings from life in a series of portrait medals, the most famous of which is a self portrait in the British Museum.

A scrapbook is a useful design aid. You can collect material that is linked by themes which you can use in design or art work. Here are some examples that you might find useful: figures; buildings; consumer products; advertising typefaces; containers; patterns; colour; and of course, subjects of your own. All of these can be supplemented by original material, such as photographs, drawings or real samples.

Perspective

Piranesi was a skilled draughtsman who turned his studies in perspective into a series of fantastic imaginary creations. He was a Venetian who learnt the skills of perspective illusion from the theatrical trickery of the Venetian theatrical painters. When he went to live in Rome he quickly established himself as one of the foremost experts on the ruins of ancient Rome. Through his studies of the

Look at the way other cultures create impressions of space in pictures. How important is it that pictures have this quality of depth? Aerial perspective uses the idea that colour and tone changes as you see greater distances, the blue of distant mountains for example. Examine paintings of distant landscapes (you may find them in the background of other pictures) for examples of this.

Giambattista Piranesi (c.1720–1778) Carceri (Prisons) plate III, *etching British Museum, London.*

ruins, his illustrations in the form of architectural drawings and his interest in the discovery of new ruins, he developed a fascinating world of inventions.

These he published as etchings, many of the plates he worked on with his own hands. He viewed the gutted ruin of the ancient city as a series of imaginary prisons. Flights of stairs, bridges, chains and ropes loop through the vaults. Here is a nightmare world made real by Piranesi's command of the perspective illusion.

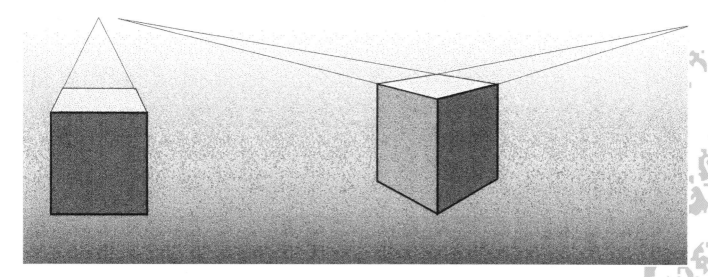

When two sides of a cube can be seen, only a single vanishing point is required.

When three sides of a cube are visible two vanishing points are required: along the horizon or at eye level.

Linear perspective is a device for creating the illusion of three dimensional space on a flat surface. Since the rediscovery of this type of space during the early Renaissance it has been the most common way for artists in the western tradition to create this illusion. It is so frequently used that it is sometimes thought to be the only way to show depth, though clearly this is not the case.

Perspective works on the basic premiss that objects appear smaller as they get further away. In the case of parallel lines these appear to meet on the horizon. The level of the horizon is determined by your eye level.

Pictures of great complexity have been created to exploit the illusion of space that the application of simple perspective rules creates. We are so used to seeing space depicted in this way that we find the devices adopted by other cultures, for example the Japanese, hard to accept. The rigid application of these rules is however a great mistake for it leads to an unreal, frozen quality in a painting. The great artists who 'managed' perspective in their pictures avoid this by using perspective judiciously and by using other space creating devices.

The Work Process

These pages look at the way making works of art can be approached. They give a series of examples. You will work out your own methods, based on your own experience. These pages do not, therefore, tell you what to do.

The painting by Spencer Gore shows how pure, simplified colour and composition can replace a straight-forward landscape. The bright colours, used freely, give a new view. The illusion of depth in the painting is created by the range of tones used. This use of colour appears again in a series of book jackets produced by Batsford Books in the 1930s. It is not suggested that the works are related, but the ideas certainly are. These two pictures demonstrate how easily ideas translate from one medium to another and from one time and place to another.

Almost all ideas that might claim to be original have some root in our visual experience. It is more often the way we use ideas that is original. The more picture images we see, the clearer we will be able to visualise our own work. This can make us more selective.

It is possible to look for help and inspiration in the work of other artists. As artists and designers, you need to be ready to look at works from other times and other cultures.

Spencer Gore (1878–1914) The Cinder Path, *1912, oil on canvas, 65.6 cm × 78.7 cm, Tate Gallery, London*

ENGLISH VILLAGE HOMES

SYDNEY R. JONES

ENGLISH VILLAGE HOMES

BATSFORD

SYDNEY R. JONES

BRIAN COOK

Brian Cook Cover Design for English Village Homes *by Sydney R. Jones, published by Batsford, 1936*

Derby biscuit porcelain group Virgins awakening Cupid *c.1790, based on a painting by Angelica Kaufman (1741–1801), University of Liverpool Art Gallery*

Proof that this happens can be seen in the way ideas have travelled the world. An example is the influence of Japanese woodblock prints on 19th century French painters. If you look in the background of some of Vincent Van Gogh's portraits for example, you will see some of his favourites pinned to the wall.

The most valuable resources are those which you can see as originals. This puts you in direct touch with the artist in a way no reproduction can. Copies of John Constable's picture *The Haywain* are very common, but only contact with the original will tell you about the texture and quality of the paint.

Work that you can see in galleries, museums or country houses is of most value if you have some idea before you go there of what you want to see. A general overview of a collection can be useful but it is better to go and look at particular items. Be prepared to take notes, make sketches or even tape-record your impressions. Colour reproductions are a poor way to look at an artist's work for they often lack correct colour and size.

Within the context of most GCSE examinations it is acceptable to use secondary material. It is *not* acceptable simply to copy a photograph or reproduction.

The translation of a piece of work from one medium to another is often an interesting exercise. This porcelain group by Angelica Kaufman shows her interest in classical subject matter. She came to England with her father at the age of 25. She is an important early female artist, one of the first to gain recognition in the country, being a founder member of The Royal Academy in London.

Henry Fuseli (1741–1825) Self Portrait 1777–79, *black and white chalks, 32.2 × 49.8 cm, National Portrait Gallery, London*

WHAT IS DRAWING?

Drawing can help you to:

- *collect information and pass it on to others.*
- *discover the world around you. It can help you learn to see.*
- *express your feelings. As many drawing techniques are fast and simple to use, you can react quickly.*
- *work out ideas, to develop those ideas and to make plans to carry them out.*

COLLECTING

Before the invention of photography at the end of the 19th century the only way to make a lasting visual record was to draw and paint. Explorers took artists with them to record their great voyages who would systematically record plant, animal and bird discoveries. An example of this type of work can be found in the *Birds of America* by J.J. Audubon. Journeys within Europe were often recorded by artists specially commissioned for the task but many also travelled on their own account, as part of the search for the 'Sublime and picturesque'. An example of this is J.M.W. Turner's journeys down the Rhine, Meuse and Mosel rivers. Later artists became more interested in the people and the exotic societies that it was in vogue to visit. Eugene Delacroix's Morocco sketchbooks clearly show this. As a record, the pictures produced by First World War artists are second to none in helping us to understand the hell they found themselves in. The official war artists' paintings can be seen in The Imperial War Museum. All these examples show how artists have produced a drawn record and passed it on to us.

DISCOVERING

Often an artist will draw to discover exactly what an object or person looks like; the exact proportions of an object need to be 'measured' for a drawing. The more frequently you make 'objective' drawings the better you train your eye to make these judgements. The more detail you discover as you draw, the more you see when you look at the world about you. Michaelangelo made many figure drawings to work out the correct anatomy for the figures in his Sistine Chapel Ceiling. Canaletto made many different figure drawings and used them to populate his paintings. If you look at his work closely you will see how Canaletto had developed his sense of observation, catching people in real, rather than contrived poses. The economy of line used by an artist like Matisse in his figure drawing, developed from an understanding of his subjects based on his skills of observation.

DESCRIPTIVE

Drawing can often help you work out ideas perhaps by scribbling on a piece of paper or maybe with more complex drawn plans. You might scribble directions or a diagram to show how some piece of machinery works, but a map or a set of drawings from a maintenance manual shows how complex and detailed drawings can become.

The first map makers were often artists combining the mappers bird's-eye view with sketches of landmarks and important details. Many of the great artists like Michaelangelo and Leonardo da Vinci drew maps, but their designs for fortifications are also well known. By tracing complex geometric shapes they produced a drawing which could then be used by engineers in constructing a building.

Architects combine the skills of the artist with the more precise drawing skills required to build their conceptions. Often they are asked to visualise their finished buildings, which we may see as an 'artistic impression'. Nowadays computer simulation can be used to give a 'virtual' picture of a proposed building, both inside and out.

EXPRESSIVE DRAWING

Some artists can draw in such a way that they share their feelings with you. Artists like Piranesi drag you down the corridors of Roman prisons, while you can fly with artists like Tiepolo whose angels and saints cruise cloud-borne about the paper.

The often sinister world of Goya propels you just as effectively in the opposite direction, his visions of the hell of Spanish resistance to Napoleon express all the pain and suffering of his time and place.

These artists work in such a way as to demand direct access to your feelings which is something that more elaborate paintings often do.

ACKNOWLEDGEMENTS

Cover and title page illustration; from *Morocco Sketchbook* by Delacroix.
(Musée Conde, Chantilly. Photograph Giraudon.)

The authors and publishers would like to thank the following individuals, institutions and companies who have given permission to reproduce photographs in this book. Every effort has been made to trace and acknowledge ownership of copyright. The publishers would be glad to make suitable arrangements with any copyright holder whom it has not been possible to contact.

AKG, London (21 bottom); Graphische Sammlung Albertina, Vienna (6); Photograph © Art Institute of Chicago. All Rights Reserved. (19 top); Batsfords Books 1936 (29 top); Bridgeman Library/Tate Gallery (17 left); British Museum (13, 17 right, 20, 26, 31 both); Copyright © Frederick Warne & Co 1987 (14, 15 both); Courtauld Institute Galleries, London (Seilern Bequest 1978) (23); Fitzwilliam Museum, University of Cambridge (12, 18); Courtesy of The Fogg Art Museum Harvard University Art Museums, Gift of Meta and Paul J Sachs © Henry Moore Foundation (5); Hirmer Archive, Munich (21); Ital Design (8 bottom); J.M. Dent and Sons (10); John Murray and Sons/Sotherbys (4); Oeffentliche Kuntsammlung Basel Kupferstichkabinett/Martin Buhler © ADAGP Paris and DACS London 1995 (16); Louvre, Paris (25); The Masters and Fellows of Magdelene College, Cambridge (24 both); The Metropolitan Museum of Art, Purchase 1924 Joseph Pulitzer Bequest (24.197.2) Copyright © 1980 by The Metropolitan Museum of Art (11 right); © Henry Moore Foundation (7); National Portrait Gallery (30); The Royal Collection © 1995 Her Majesty Queen Elizabeth II (11 left); Tate and Lyle Sugars (8 top); Tate Gallery (19 left); Uffizi Gallery/SCALA (9); University of Liverpool Art Galleries (29 bottom); Witt Library, Courtauld Institute Galleries, London (22); Yale University Art Gallery, Evertt V. Meeks Fund (3).

For Dianne and Serena

British Library Cataloguing in Publication Data

Dunn, Chris
    Drawing. – (Art & Design Series)
    I. Title   II. Series
    741

ISBN 0 340 532769

First published 1995
Impression number   10 9 8 7 6 5 4 3 2 1
Year   1999   1998   1997   1996   1995

Typeset by Wearset, Boldon, Tyne and Wear.
Printed in Great Britain for Hodder & Stoughton Educational, a division of Hodder Headline Plc, 338 Euston Road, London NW1 3BH by Cambus Litho Ltd, East Kilbride.